HEART
of the
DESERT

A collection of poetic healing, searching for meaning and rediscovering peace

MONTE J HANKS
Vietnam Veteran

Featuring original watercolors by Jessica Hanks Kaserman

Copyright © 2023 Monte J Hanks

All rights reserved. No portion of this book may be preproduced in any form without written permission from the author.

Book cover designed by Merry Robin Publishing, LLC

Featuring original watercolor artwork by Jessica Hanks Kaserman. Copyright for artwork © 2023 Jessica Hanks Kaserman

1st Edition

Library of Congress Control Number: 2023921167

Published in partnership with Merry Robin Publishing, LLC

To explore more of our published works, please visit www.Life-OnPurpose.com/Books

Paperback ISBN: 978-1-962975-00-1
Hardcover ISBN: 978-1-962975-01-8

*This collection of poems is dedicated to Tiffiny,
my first reader, partner and wife,
who supports my desire to continue writing.
She is always present,
encouraging me to remember my dream,
stop doubting and move on!*

Thank you, my love.

CRADLE

The red desert,
she holds me close in her cradle of rocks.

The mystery of my attraction
returns me again and again to this place of
remembrance.

To be in the presence of earth's wonders
evokes the true nature of my spirit.

Some time before,
I was held closer to the healing power of red
dirt
and I imagine my blood would pour red dust if
exposed to the sun!

To feel the sensuous curve of rock
beneath my hands
connects me to all that has been and will be.

From this land my strength returns,
reminds me of who I am.
As it whispers secrets,
I feel my soul breathe deep.

When I am surrounded by artificial life
within city walls,
I dream of blue skies and clear air
running through my veins,

freeing me to dwell with the 'Great Spirit'
who holds all.

A watcher in the rocks am I,
as The Watcher waits for me.

CONTENTS

Cradle	i
Introduction	1
Ink Pictures	7
Dream Valley	8
Backyard Mentor	10
Harmony	12
Desert Spirits	13
Creek Peace	14
Time Before Time	16
Old Spruce	18
Re-Entry Burns	19
Fishing for Life	20
Memories Trailing Desires	22
Soul Light	24
Past Visions	25
Becoming	28
The Dolores River	30
Liquid Life	32

Stone	33
Lunar Dreams	34
On the Water	36
Time Lapse	38
Sanctuary	41
Haiku	42
The Correct Order of Things	43
Unheard...	46
Red Desert on the 3rd Planet from the Sun	48
Acknowledgements	52
About the Author	55
About the Artist	57
Locations	59
Recommended Reading	64

INTRODUCTION

I have come to believe that we have many lives within our one life on this planet.

As I have grown older, I look back and wonder who I was during different chapters of my history. It started out beautifully as a child and young boy. And, as happens in life, changes came that pulled me under for a time—war, substance abuse, self-sabotaged relationships, disconnect from family—lost dreams turned into lost years. I became someone I did not recognize nor care for. By some miracle, I discovered a path that brought me *home*.

After serving in the army and spending some time in Vietnam, I became very disillusioned. I attempted to make sense of that insanity, gave up and numbed out for the next 20 years, relying on alcohol and drugs to carry me through the days. I left a trail of personal wreckage, trying to forget the pain of returning home to a country ideologically divided with itself, where a young Vietnam Veteran was not respected.

Despite my addictions, I found work doing various jobs in construction, equipment operator, oil field rig-up trucks, ranch-hand, long-haul truck driving and more. They were good jobs and honest work, but I was distracted, only focused on "making a buck" and perhaps proving to myself that I was still a man after the disappointment of coming home.

I learned to mask every emotion except anger as it seemed to be the only socially acceptable emotion for men, and it provided protection from ridicule and ignorance. My descent into darkness was a result of this suppression combined with the various forms of trauma from the war. I struggled with my father's and society's version of what a man is supposed to be: men don't cry and that feeling emotional was for women. Fortunately, after 20 years of living in the shadows, I had my wake up call.

My father passed away and something stirred in me. I took a hard look in the mirror and decided I was not invincible. Nine months after he died (attributed to alcoholism), I stopped my self-destructive spiral. I returned to college at forty-one seeking a career that was personally fulfilling. In an English literature class, our professor directed us to write a poem and even keep a journal! After a collective groan from all of the men, I started journaling, writing some rough poetry, and discovered myself on the page.

I looked deeper into what it meant to me to be a man. I was trying to reconnect with myself and face the problems I had avoided. Eventually, I discovered a supportive men's group. We talked about family, work, respect, integrity, and our role in life.

More importantly, for me, we expressed how we felt without reproach. We learned that we could still provide and be a protector, but not "to sell ourselves short," and deny our true feelings. We shared our day-to-day struggles, our fears, and our often-stifled creativity. The musicians of the group shared songs and many of us shared poetry. Poetry became a consistent feature of our meetings due to the insights it provided of our deepest beliefs and feelings. With their support, my poetry blossomed.

I evolved into someone I did not recognize. I began to read poetry from Mary Oliver, Rumi, Walt Whitman, Lawrence Ferlinghetti, Edward Abbey, William Stafford, Pablo Neruda and more. One book in particular made its mark on me, The Rag & Bone Shop Of The Heart, Poems for Men.

These poets spoke to me, especially how they were able to connect with themselves as they discovered, explored, and loved the world. Many Native authors had a direct impact on my writing as well, including N. Scott Momaday, Leslie Marmon Silko, Joy Harjo, Sherman Alexi, Dee Brown, Simon Oritz and more.

Poetry opened doors and connected me to something far greater than my human experience. My heart calmed as the words circling in my mind landed on the page. I can't quite explain what changed, but I knew I wanted to feel what other writers felt and why they wrote what they wrote. My journey towards writing this collection was born of a desire to recover my heart and soul. A perfect description of my sojourn comes from Mary Oliver's poem, "The Journey."

From the first line, "One day you finally knew what you had to do, and began," to, "there was a new voice that you slowly recognized as your own," and the last line, "determined to save the only life that you could save," her words resonated with me on a profound level.

The poems in this collection were inspired from travels into the mountains of Utah, Idaho, Wyoming and Montana, but mostly from Southern Utah's red rock country. Some arrived after time spent in nature, and others *insisted* on being created in the moment. "Cradle" describes my thoughts every time I was in the desert where I felt safe and home. "Sanctuary" was conceived from camping next to the Colorado River off Potash Road, outside of Moab in 1997, during the Comet Hale-Bopp. It was a glorious sight as the comet appeared to sail between the stone red sentinels which left us breathless as if stunned by magic. "Timelapse" takes place in the middle of a winter's night between Boulder and Torrey, Utah. I was watching the moon and found myself shuffling in a small circle to keep pace, as if I was standing on earth's axis.

These times in nature expanded my limited view of existence on a human level, and I was often reminded of the endless universe compared to the beating of one tiny human heart. To put it plainly, it was an ongoing spiritual awakening, sometimes difficult to describe with mere words. Some things cannot be explained. They must be lived ... or put into a poem.

You will find a recurring theme of awakening/healing and references to our "Red Mother," "Grand Mother" and "Great Spirit."

I felt that this was the appropriate and respectful way to describe "guardian spirits" that are the connection between humans, earth and all that dwells upon it and what should guide our hand in nature. My friendship with Albert Tinhorn & Katchee Eli Mitchell of the Navajo Nation grew my interest in native culture. I had opportunities to participate in sweat lodges and cultural events with different tribes, and it shaped many of my poems. You will see the impact of this, particularly in my poems "Becoming" and "Past Visions." I will be forever grateful to the Dine' who were part of my healing process by being the first people who honored me as a Vietnam Veteran. We have a lot to learn about honor, integrity, and respect from them.

There is beauty and life everywhere, created by the natural world. The red desert, especially, gave me a renewed sense of being and purpose. It is my prayer that these poems will shed light on one person's journey back to life and perhaps touch your heart. I often felt an *energy,* a *spirit* dwelling among the sacred places I roamed. Perhaps it was Earth and the "Great Spirit" speaking to me . . . now that I am listening.

May these poems from my heart connect with yours.

Sweet journey, my friends.

—Monte J Hanks

INK PICTURES

He drags his books and papers behind him
wherever he goes.
Well intentioned, seeking inspiration.

No forest or desert,
lake or river
is safe.

He pulls the ink from earth's well,
pours it on the page.
Some clarity captures the moment.

Most, vain attempts at deciphering her message.
The casual tourist 'clicks' away his vacation on film.

The writer snickers,
pen stuck to the page.

Beauty marches past,
oblivious of our ideas,
ongoing and endless,
waiting for you to join its rhythm.

We scurry by,
intent on looking
but not seeing.

The world seems to be accelerating, people say.

Or is it us,
rushing to get nowhere, faster?
Feet and tires spinning the globe quicker?

Lust for more of everything,
turning our heads round and round.

Never satisfied with what has been given.

DREAM VALLEY

This morning I left again.

The valley of my dreams,
the soul of my desire
is without me.

Who misses the other more?

Did I leave a trace of myself
floating between the red canyon walls,
waiting for the morning birds
to sing in memory?

Who misses more?

We travel the north road,
leading to another shift in reality.

These small sorties once satisfied my hunger.
Now, my dream life is traveling
faster than before.

Brief passages into my depths
lit the candle of remembering.

Heart of the Desert

What was thought or imagined is
burning, arcing higher,
pushing the false moons aside,
revealing the lost universe
where my journey began.

The black hole is mending.
The sacred valley I am seeking,
imagined to be where I am not,
has been within a heart's reach,
always.

As I open myself to infinite life,
I see through new eyes.

The one who is missing is I.

The gods merely await our awakening,
presenting the earth's beauty
to replenish our hungry souls.

BACKYARD MENTOR

Under the apple tree,
waiting for inspiration,
I wasn't aware
I just needed motivation.

Over-head,
the twisted old tree
waited with patience.
It has withstood time
with honor and elegance.

Canyon winds have not rocked its roots.
Snow is shrugged off,
preparing for fruit.

Thunder and hail have dropped a few leaves
and yet, it stands in the cool evening breeze.

I never heard it complain,
except when I trimmed to tight,
Unlike my whining about obstacles
that keep me up at night.

The tree merely sways
within nature's force
and sings of its happiness
to be close to the source.

The trunk and its branches
created sacred space
Where resilience and growth
move with grace.

I am blessed by this tree
beyond measure
And I am grateful I am alive
to reap its treasure.

HARMONY

Of soft afternoons in the pines by the endless river

Of food and drink shared under the trees

Of sunlight gracing the pages of a book

Of laughter and thoughts and intimacy

Of birds singing and animals talking

The dog romps up the trail
to greet life in all its beauty.

Magical days when the clock is put away
and time is enjoyed in the present.

Listening to the earth,
our false, created world slips away,
Our souls refilled with truth.

Will we remember to keep it in our hearts upon returning?

Can we take the music of the river home to sustain peace?

Of all our efforts to progress,
all we will take back
is what has filled our hearts.

DESERT SPIRITS

Scrubby little green spirits
stationed on the desert floor,
offering safe haven for small critters.

They watch the movers
scurry around their shores.

The cacti crowd lays in wait
ambushing bumbling invaders
who awaken too late.

Ravines and gullies flow to destinations.

Purple rocks planted to alter courses
redirect wind and water
to keep up social graces.

Petrified priest and nuns
guard their cracked castle,
tolerating short visits of
movers and flyers who dare.

The vast, pulsating sky enshrouds all,
pre-ordained by gods of those places.

CREEK PEACE

I love to hear the creek speak
as it rolls down the canyon,
delivering peace from the nervous city.
I walk and listen to nothing.
Everything.

The water asks, 'Why do you not visit often?
We are as close as a tranquil thought.'
The trees nod their approval
as they whisper in harmony
with the water's lullaby.

'It's a blessing to hear your voices,' I reply.
The city's sirens and smog-bound valley
held me captive for too long,
but my heart hears your call.
Always.

The pulse within joins life rushing onward,
enchants the rhythm we share.
I am amazed and grateful of nature's presence
and how she continues
to stitch my soul together again.

TIME BEFORE TIME

Sometimes I grow weary and
my desire to disappear
into the red rocks
accelerates.

Like many before,
I consider the possibility of life beyond humans,
pure existence in the hands of Red Mother.
Nothing feels this good.

Just give me a month, a few precious weeks, a day,
some present time to pass inward,
to lose myself to find myself
for the chance to rise again,
to weed out frivolous thoughts
that drive us to an early plot.

Heart of the Desert

Stone red sentinels wait for my choice.
They demand nothing . . . everything.
To stand in their midst is to arrive at heaven's gate.
I have been close,
but the world brought me back.
Escape is unlikely, but another year has passed.

A half-century mortal,
insignificant,
standing at the foot of immortal stone
on this sacred world.

The old channels are opening and await rebirth.
My life is half over and I have yet
to gain a foothold in my own landscape,
to explore what is already there.

Sand pours through the hourglass of this millennium,
slipping through my fingers.
Unless I find the key to my elusive door,
I will wait for this body to pass, freeing me at last.

OLD SPRUCE

Stump is all that's left.

Wind took our old friend,
a sentinel at the corner of our home
and guardian of the local quail.

Grass is naked.

Pine needle burial mound remains.
Wood split to warm the home.
Romantic notions left the stump with
roots attached.

Future foundation for a garden table
or a special place surrounded by flowers.

We care for old friends.

RE-ENTRY BURNS

Out of the desert beauty,
into the hard-lined city
noise and confusion.

Awakened memories
from the other world,
or is it just today?

Have I betrayed my soul
 returning to these walls?

It screams for the freedom
to experience the vast silence.

Struggling,
on the verge of tears,
not sure how I arrived at this juncture.

My heart lives for the balance of red rocks
under blue skies,
endless horizons that beckon me home.

Is this my path to wholeness
between hallowed land and the city?

Reality fractures.

Desert burns on and I,
inspired by its endurance,
will not accept less.

FISHING FOR LIFE

If you watch the river long enough,
the desire to leap quickens.

Standing on the edge of earth
watching endless currents,
waiting for trout to rise,
feeding energy in my line,
through my hand,
instantly making us one
with the river of life.

Who watches the earth turn
around the rivers that play by our feet?

Are their thoughts ours
and what can they tell us of this cycle?

Have we forgotten
ancient memories that will return
peace to our spirit
and leave imagined lives on the bank?

Heart of the Desert

Tempting to live with the fish,
seeking simple knowledge
of our existence,
beyond man's interference
and self-importance.

The answer lives within us.

The simple joy of throwing
a lifeline to nature,

not to destroy,
but to connect

and give back,

replenishes my soul.

MEMORIES TRAILING DESIRES

The great plains industrial city,
bred from old west legends,
simmers.

Coal trains hammer the night.
Jets rip across ridges.

Hotels and smokestacks
scrape the sullen sky.

Streets support combustion
as people rush
to pay for city life.

In every shop,
the pride of their land,
pictures,
paintings,
photos
and cards,
events of days gone by.

While here,
the nuts,
bolts
and gears
churn
a choking death.

We shrug our shoulders,
fuel our tanks.

In our bones of bones,
a small shudder.

Primal instincts awakened as the
earth rolls over
and the old star
fills our eyes with memories.

SOUL LIGHT

The sun builds a bridge
across the Great Salt Lake.

Golden shadows
caress the path of light.

Its shimmering essence
awakens the sleeper within me.

The light narrows,
disappears,
glides back to lure my eyes,
coaxing my spirit
to step into its warmth.

My mind sees mirages on the water.

My heart receives illumination,
restoring peace.

Simple pleasures
softening defenses
focused,
remembering,
within nature's arms.

A safe place is all we seek,
all we need.

PAST VISIONS I

My eyes perceive vast reaches of land.

This vision from Boulder Mountain
stretches my mind beyond the cities' rush
to soften hard edges of humans 'doing.'

Capitol Reef's ancestral red ridges,
white plateaus and the distant purple-black
Henry Mountains resurrect my being.

My soul shakes city residue from its shoulders.

The bitter taste of smog
exhales from my lungs,
replenished with the exotic flavor
of blue sky.

My heart yearns to witness the beauty,
the gift of creation.

This earth and I,
we struggle to survive
the onslaught of my kind,
lost creatures with one goal:

to control and own
what spirit has offered
to revere and honor.

Everything we need surrounds
our stone-blind eyes
while greedy,
misplaced desires destroy
or abandon life,
molesting this world
to satisfy fantasies.

PAST VISIONS II

One foot is stuck in the material world
of convenience and false security,

paid for
with sweat,
pain
and a lifetime of sacrifice

wasted
at money's corrupt,
golden altar.

The earth feels it
—the rape of our home-
the desecration of our souls and
I rage at our naiveté!

The other foot is free on Boulder Mountain
and Abbey's sacred deserts
that breathe
and sing of life,

beyond the affliction of steel,
concrete and glass-paneled
symbols of success.

This foot will dance, sing
and treasure the gift of life,

will celebrate
each breath
and give thanks
for the time
the other foot rises
out of misery
to dance
lightly
on our home.

BECOMING

How do I tell you how I feel . . .
becoming one with the power of the desert?

Sandstone,
slickrock,
cacti,
cedar,
fragile soil
on delicate rock.

How could I possibly hope for you to hear how I am
becoming . . .

every glimmer of sun until I am the rock you think you see,
becoming . . .

the wind, carving out heavenly shapes
for the sheer pleasure of creation.

Feeling her caress,
I am whole,
home again with my companion.

Heart of the Desert

Rocks speaking to my bones,
earth speaking to my body,
cottonwood leaves glowing in the sun,
sparkle of dew,
creek bed full of rain,
blood pumping through my veins!

I feel her message of life,
allowing me into her arms
where my body is her body,
my heart,
the spring from which
her rivers run free.

Come and sit with me.

Can you not feel her caress of breath?
Does she not let us lie on her breasts and heal?
Does she not wash and feed us?
Does she not wait for us to love her as she loves us?

We belong to The Grand Mother . . .
and how we care for ourselves
is how we care for her.

THE DOLORES RIVER

We slip through a chute of mad water,
feel the brace of cold wash over!

Another worry overboard.

We round the boulder from cliffs above
to open onto smooth water.

The pressure drops another notch.

Ahead, more boiling rapids
roaring with double dares!

Run me if you can!

Test your life against my power.
We run, we survive.

Another worry floats away.

The magic river pulls my walls down, one by one.
As we drop through the gorges, my fever cools.

City, job, money, sink below.

This is my life!
The river calls.

Come flow with me and release your pain.

There is only me and there is only you.
Push the intruders away
before they bleed you dry.

Their world is false.

Do not forget your power.

Do not wait in their backwater pools of muddied dreams
nor lie complacent within their eddies that lead nowhere.

Oh, my endless river of life,
feel my soul loving you!

LIQUID LIFE

Liquid life floats off the edge of the red universe,
feeding the earth from time immemorial.

A recent life form stands in awe of the mystery
while the elements of creation continue infinite cycles.

The ancients knew the wisdom that guides this rhythm.
If we listened, we would heed their lessons.

The storm tumbles from the heavens,
bursts onto the blue planet.

Cleansing and renewal bring new growth,
as it has from the beginning.

This blessed liquid surrounds
and lives within our private temples,
transports us in our journey through millennia.

Where red monoliths join with the pools and roots,
white fire and fluid seed pursue young embryos!

A lucid world sought by the living,
swimming through eternal secrets
to feel the pulse that connects all.

STONE

I have always been
and will be.

Passing bipeds
have pecked upon me,
excavating for imagined treasures.

Others worshiped my impossible heights.

Everything comes and goes.

I remain.

Before water concealed my rising mass,
I dwelled within earth's womb.

Volcanic shifts thrust me
above her protection.

Fragile creatures disappeared,
others adapted.

But I remain.

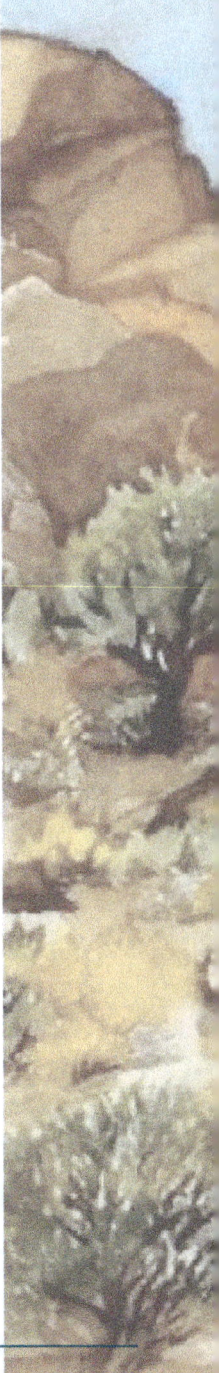

LUNAR DREAMS

The earth revolves
and the daystar snubs
that glorious moon.

Why it disturbs my sleep is a mystery.

The moon and I are confidantes,
sharing secrets of the illusion.

That loud, yellow orb
creates too much havoc for my taste.

I prefer to sail on lunar light,
slipping my vision ship
through the wake of comets,
chasing their tails,
circling planets,
canvas filling for the jump,
gravity accelerating us to the center,
slinging my vessel beyond the beyond . . .

Velocity,
rate of motion related to time,
vectoring in the speed of light,
trajectory altered and

I sail right through my life!

ON THE WATER

On the water,
amidst stone red walls
parting the sky.

The surface below my own walls stand,
.entrenched.

Personal monuments of Homo erectus'
struggle to understand self against barriers of granite.

›Unmovable‹

Now, the *erosion* of years softens the rock.

Granules
       of
          sand
              trickle
                   down
                          exposing raw life beneath.
Another ancient thought

            b r e a k s
                   o   f   f
                           s
                           i
                           n
                           k
                           s
                            below the surface.

Time works the bre ak,
preparing for survival.

A fragment remains exposed

. . . breathing . . .

The shroud recedes.

Light awakens the seed
and the alchemist brews the mix.

Original thinking b ^{en}ds around New Laws!

Decay ^{up}roots itself,
creating multiple perceptions in its wake.

Life is re-defining

experiencing endlesssssssssssssssssssssssssssssssssssssss

d i *men* S i o n s .

TIME LAPSE

'She' spins,
causing my feet to turn in small steps,
keeping time.

I exist for this moment on a quiet,
cold winter's eve
upon the mountain's belly
between her blouse of pine
and the boulders
spread below her skirt of snow.

I evolve with the earth
while that half moon witch
speeds across the universe.

A desperate entourage of stars strain to stay the trail.

I find my body out there,
rolling out of earth's rhythm,
desiring communion with her.

She seduces my being,
a siren of forever,
gathering souls within her tides
of pale white magic,
reeling us deeper in her grasp,
racing on endless star paths.

Heart of the Desert

Our destiny,
our ultimate journey's end
known only to her and the
far reaches of my estranged body
and I am released,
set free,

as every particle of what was me
restores this mystical spirit
and spirals outward!

Each fiber of existence imagines itself into a being
that I could only dream,
but has remained within,
never losing awareness of its true form,
concealed until this moment on a clean winter's night,
gathering...

gathering more of me,
a force,
a huge kindness within/without,
calling me home!

My feet stumble to stay with the body
spinning off this mountain pass,
beyond what I have known.

. . . and the car door closes.

I stagger,
dismissed into what I was
as my companion waits in the warm machine.

I stand within the heart of this mountain,
sadly watching the half moon
continue the course of another time
and I am not me . . .

I am forever altered
and
I remember.

SANCTUARY

Oh, we struggle,
leaving the desert.

Its soul is our soul
and our hearts fall to the red dirt,
heavy as the stone that lost earth's footings
to rest where it may.

Last eve we watched the comet
trail over the edge of red monoliths
and disappear into the universe.

From beneath our canopy of stars,
giant shadows met the night above.

We heard the call of geese
flying up the great river
seeking safe haven from the night.

Fire warms our bodies
as we stare into space and dream.

Our hearts are with the geese
as they search for home.

We have found ours and
oh, but we loathe to leave this sanctuary!

HAIKUS

Scrubby green life squats
The cacti crowd lays in wait
Small critters escape

Desert spirits wait
Tolerate visits too late
But guard against snakes

Red desert gives grace
Holds a place within our hearts
Settles city clamor

THE CORRECT ORDER OF THINGS
I.

The trees rise straight,
strong and true,
as if to lift
the weight of the world.

As tender saplings,
they heard
the sky calling.

Seedling seeks water to split.

Taproot works the soil.

Stem expands to the air.

Once rooted in earth,
then tracking
the moon,
stars
and the sun.

THE CORRECT ORDER OF THINGS II.

We exist, fearing death.

Learning why/how
to live.

Crawling,
walking,
running,
absorbing knowledge

to stand upright.

Slowly,
blessedly,
experiencing love,

nurtured to create.

THE CORRECT ORDER OF THINGS III.

Prayers before movement,
bodies stretching,
thoughts ever-expanding.

We rise to
find our place
in the Universe.

What we bring
touches everyone.

Will it be peace
or turmoil?

thought before speaking,

reflection before reaction.

UNHEARD . . .

I had not heard that before,
perhaps never noticed.

A soft, cushioned whump,
some gravity behind it.

Pen stumbled, fingers faltered.

A small disturbance
barely registered in an
otherwise occupied mind.

Reverie broken, resurfacing
amid hushed,
fellow creatures
immersed in reading
others' imaginings
while residing in a time
less than a cosmic blink,
yet consumed by simple
comprehension
of immediate environs.

Primal instinct scans for the source,
bypassing the wobbly-legged table
balanced with the morning's
coffee pot, pans and discarded scraps,

> to settle briefly
> on the annual
> miracle of
> cacti blooms,

and onward
over the broken boulders
once drowned by oceans
too old to remember,

> to arrive, dazed,
> at the sight of a
> tiny lizard,
> tongue testing dry air,

> freshly plopped
> in the sand
> from an adventure
> on our cooking rocks.

Leathery body
performs four-legged "push-ups"
from some ancient memory

> to bring me home
> to a quiet reality I prefer.

RED DESERT ON THE 3RD PLANET FROM THE SUN

The red desert thaws this winter morning.
Silver pods of frost bounce off fence posts
outside the cabin window,
chasing scrub jays from pole to pole.

The morning sun reveals ancient formations
that burst above earths' surface,
creating a mystical world
of spires, mesas, plateaus and canyons.

Wind and water carved waves of red and purple stone
that welcome us to the mystery.
And we, recently free of the city clamor,
are stunned into silence.

Just a few greeting birds,
as our feet fall upon the earth we share,
but forget is there, waiting to replenish
our deep, deep soul of remembering.

Heart of the Desert

Ancient memories tug at the edge of awareness
attempting to connect with the desert
on the third planet from the sun,
spinning through the endless universe.

What do we offer this blue planet?

What will our ego-focused endeavors
finally create when the dust
of our mad progression settles?

We are reborn
within the grace of red desert
and don't really know why

but instead,
we bask in its illuminating beauty
and hold a place in our hearts
wherever we wander.

The frost has melted.

The scrub jays have flown
and we live again,
walking gently,
hand in hand
upon our home.

ACKNOWLEDGEMENTS

I did not arrive at this point to publish my first book of poetry without the help and support of many people. Not all are still with us, but nevertheless, they have my gratitude.

Holly and Jayne Ann of Merry Robin Publishing have been a blessing, and I am still in awe of their expertise, creativity, support, and guidance to bring this book to life.

A big thanks to my friend, Dr. Craig McManama, who (upon learning of my writing) directed me to his daughter, Megan, who referred me to Holly and Jayne Ann.

I give my ongoing gratitude to Jessica for the art she created for my poems. I asked her to read them and paint what she saw, and she did just that, perfectly.

To my friend, brother veteran and mentor, Tom Cleary, who is still educating me about the world (& forms) of poetry and whom I performed poetry with in SLC. Thank you for always being there.

To Ben Cabey, another fellow poet in our performance poetry group, passed on now. He taught me the art of performing.

God bless.

I owe a debt of gratitude to the men's group in SLC for their support and encouragement and especially our member, Florin R. Nielsen, poet extraordinaire, who has also passed on. He was a gentleman with class and compassion.

I want to recognize Rebecca, my former wife, who recently passed on just before publishing this book. She was my camping partner on the many excursions we made into the mountains and deserts and was present when I was inspired to write many of the poems in this collection.

Thanks to my friends who first introduced me to Utah's deserts and the great times we had in red rock country. Who knew it would end up with me creating poetry, eh Jim Hunter?

I am compelled to honor the Spirit (Spirits?) that never gave up and have gently guided me. (Well, not always gently, but I need a hard nudge from time to time.) I am blessed and grateful that I am listening and coming full circle.

A'ho!

ABOUT THE AUTHOR

Monte has walked several decades of his life's journey, and time has diverted him down roads of disappointment, anger, and at times ultimate despair. But it has also been filled with gratitude, growth, and a discovery of self. The past has shaped his future, being a footprint of who he has become. At times, the twists of the journey surprise him in the direction they take. He has many experiences that demonstrate the true will of the human spirit, both personally and professionally. He is a Vietnam Veteran and that time in his life left permanent memories, some painful and others full of gratitude.

After his time in the military, he struggled with substance abuse, eventually overcoming that dark period of his life. For 20 years he worked a variety of jobs just trying to survive. He chose a hard path that was physically demanding. After a "wake-up call" by the death of his father, he returned to college at 41 to find a new career that was personally fulfilling.

After graduating and for the next 30 years, Monte worked with those experiencing homelessness in Salt Lake City. He created programs when other options didn't exist, establishing community relations and building collaborations, but most importantly, being present to homeless men and women to offer resources, kindness, and, above all, hope.
Monte would not say that he is self-accomplished, rather accomplishing what moves his soul. He retired this year and has returned to writing poetry and perhaps to finish a couple of books he began years ago.

His journey is changing direction, so perhaps there are more surprises yet to come.

ABOUT THE ARTIST

Many years ago, Jessica Hanks Kaserman shared the vision of this book with Monte Hanks. He presented Jessica with several poems that he was working on and asked if she would collaborate with him and paint some watercolor paintings for the book. She was honored and excited to be a part of the project.

Soon after their meeting, the collaboration began.

During the process, incredibly tragic events happened in both their lives, and the book was put aside for a while. Years later, Jessica was surprised and very excited to hear that the dream was becoming a reality. The book was finally coming together and in the process of publication.

It had been so long, she had forgotten about the original thought and the paintings. After the initial shock of the news of the publication she thought, "it's about time!"

Jessica has been painting since 1979. Her paintings are always changing. She finds excitement in different textures and techniques to incorporate into her watercolors. She finds inspiration in the beauty of nature, in the love of painting and sharing her visions.

Her watercolors are a continuing meditation of capturing her life moments in real time. For Jessica, timelines, deadlines and preparing for shows takes the joy out of the painting experience. Although she has had many showings of her work through the years, Jessica now prefers to paint for herself, her loved ones and her friends.

LOCATIONS

There are too many soul-stirring desert locations and landscapes to count. However, these are some of my personal favorites - sanctuaries of healing, light, creativity and inspiration.

Should you feel so inclined to visit any of these locations, be sure to take the time to pause and truly feel the energy and life radiating from these seemingly barren deserts. You won't be disappointed! You may even be moved to create some of your own poetry.

<u>Locations that inspired the poems in this collection:</u>

"Cradle" was inspired by my adventures in Temple Mountain area. Goblin Valley is off the same road. Access both from Hwy 24 going south from I 70.

"Harmony" was written on a camping trip by Henry's Fork of the Snake River in Island Park, Idaho.

"Dream Valley" was written from visits to Castle Valley, 16 miles northeast of Moab near State Route 128.

"Creek Peace" was sparked by adventures in Mill Creek Canyon, SLC.

"Fishing for Life" was from one of my attempts at fly fishing on the Weber River by Wanship, Utah. After numerous attempts at casting (from which the bushes reigned victorious), I gave up, sat on the bank with my feet in the water and wrote this poem.

"Memories Trailing Desires" was written when my car broke down in Billings, Montana. I had a conference there where I was presenting about respite care for homeless, a previous career.

Highway 12, between Torrey and Boulder, UT inspired "Past visions." That was about the same place I wrote "Time Lapse" - we had stopped at a scenic view turnout in the middle of nowhere.

"Liquid Life" - Lake Powell

"On the Water" - A four day river trip down the Green River.

"Soul Light" was inspired watching the sun set on the Great Salt Lake

"Sanctuary" was written off Potash Road, (Hwy 114) by the Colorado River off Hwy 89 just north of Moab.

"Red Desert: Third Planet from the Sun" was written at Kodachrome Basin State Park

"Unheard" was about a little lizard I found near Indian Canyon.

Recommended Wanderings:

Temple Mountain - I've wandered around there a lot. It doesn't look like much until you get down in there. It's just incredible.

Goblin Valley - right next to Temple

Arches, of course you can hit up the tourist spots, but don't forget to explore little pockets

Canyonlands, National Park - it's a great place to get lost in.

Monument Valley

Escalante National Monument

Dead Horse Point – Used to be a hidden treasure. Off Hwy 313 from Hwy 191. I slept overnight when there were just large boulders to prevent cars from driving off the cliff; was awoken by an irritated park ranger. This Hwy also takes you to Island in the Sky.

Indian Creek Corridor, Scenic Byway (S.R. 211) there's a turnoff, Hartpoint Road. Follow it for several miles. You will cross a couple of small creeks (if it is spring) and finally come up on a ridge where you can set up a primitive camp. In the spring, the Cacti were blooming!

And, be sure to continue west along S.R. 211 as it will take you to the Needles District of Canyonlands National Park.

Along the same highway, you will find Newspaper Rock.

Capital Reef National Park has access to some great slot canyons.

Buckhorn Wash on the Green River Cutoff road headed East off Hwy 10 just north of Castledale. Check out the Wedge Overlook off this dirt road—camped right on the edge back then. Looks over the San Rafael River.

San Rafael Swell: If you are looking for more remote areas, the 'Swell' is the area to explore. It is just below I-70, about 16 miles west of Green River.

RECOMMENDED READING

Poetry:

Mary Oliver: *my favorite poet*
Dreamwork
Westwind
Blue Horses
Felicity

Rumi:
The Essential Rumi, Translations by Coleman Barks with John Moyne
We Are Three, New Rumi Translations by Coleman Barks

The Rag and Bone Shop of the Heart, Poems for Men – a collection of world poems
Editors Robert Bly, James Hillman and Michael Meade

Joy Harjo: First Native American to be a U.S. Poet Laureate 2019-2022, Muscogee Creek Heritage, poet, writer, academic, musician and activist. Some of her poetry:
Poet Warrior
Crazy Brave
An American Sunrise
The Woman Who Fell from The Sky
She Had Some Horses

How to Paint Sunlight by Lawrence Ferlinghetti

Even in Quiet Places by William Stafford

Selected Poems by Czeslaw Milosz

Robert Bly:
Morning Poems
Loving A Woman in Two Worlds

Roger Housden, *a collection of powerful poems by international authors with his thoughts. This is a perfect book for an introduction into poems that can truly change your life:*
Ten Poems to Change Your Life
Ten Poems to Change Your Life Again and Again

After Ikkyu and other poems by Jim Harrison. He is one of my favorite authors of fiction like "Legends of the Fall," "True North," "The Big Seven," "The Great Leader"

Kahlil Gibram
Thoughts and Meditations

Books - novels, fiction, nonfiction, essays:

Edward Abbey: *His experiences in the desert and the consequent books he wrote, impacted me greatly, especially his efforts to protect the land.*
Desert Solitaire: *a must read from his experiences in the American southwestern wilderness.*
Earth Apples, his poetry, edited by David Pearson
Down the River
The Journey Home
The Fool's Progress
One Life at a Time, Please
A Voice Crying in the Wilderness: Notes from a Secret Journal
Abbey's Road
The Monkey Wrench Gang
Hayduke Lives!

Terry Tempest Williams: a Utah author, also educator, conservationist, and activist. *Her essays and books compel me to look deeper into our world. She is an amazing human being.*
Why I Write, *her essay on writing which resides on my desk.*
The Open Space of Democracy
Refuge: An Unnatural History of Family and Place
Red, Passion and Patience in the Desert
An Unspoken Hunger, Stories from the Field

Citizens Dissent by Wendell Berry & David James Duncan

Patriotism and the American Land, by Barry Lopez, Terry Tempest Williams, Richard Nelson

The Partly Cloudy Patriot by Sarah Vowell

Linda Hogan:
Dwellings
People of the Well
Power

Men and the Water of Life: Initiation, by Michael Meade

Sam Keen:
Fire In The Belly, On Being a Man
Inward Bound

The Heart Aroused, Poetry and the Preservation of the Soul in corporate America, by David Whyte

The Four Agreements by Don Miguel Ruiz

Thoughts and Meditations, Kahlil Gibran, translated and edited by Anthony R. Ferris

Prophet, Kahlil Gibran, published by Alfred A. Knopf

Paul Coelho, Brazilian lyricist and novelist:
The Pilgrimage
The Alchemist *(some call this his masterpiece)*
The Valkyries
By the River Piedra I Sat Down and Wept

Leslie Marmon Silko, Laguna Pueblo, Mexican and Anglo-American heritage—novelist and poet:
Ceremony - *a story for anyone returning from war*

N. Scott Momaday, Native Author, Kiowa—novelist, poet, essayist:
House Made of Dawn (Pulitzer Prize for fiction 1969)
The Names
The Ancient Child

Sherman Alexi, Native Author, Spokane Tribe of the Spokane Reservation, Novelist, poet, short story writer and filmmaker:
Reservation Blues
Blasphemy
The Lone Ranger and Tonto Fistfight in Heaven
War Dances
Indian Killer

Black Elk: The Sacred Ways of the Lakota by Wallace Black Elk and William S Lyon

Where the Blue Bird Sings to the Lemonade Springs by Wallace Stegner

Grizzly Years by Doug Peacock, *Vietnam Veteran whose road to recovery led through the wilderness of the Rocky Mountains. Also, said to be the character Hayduke was based on in Edward Abbey's book.*

Rick Bass, author and environmental activist:
The Skies, The Stars, The Wilderness
The Lost Grizzlies

FOR MORE...

Information about upcoming projects, how to get in touch with Monte, please visit:

www.life-onpurpose.com/MonteJHanks

If you enjoyed this collection, please be sure to share it with a friend and leave a review on Amazon.com. Small gestures like these make a world of difference for authors.

www.ingramcontent.com/pod-product-compliance
Lightning Source LLC
LaVergne TN
LVHW021120080426
835510LV00012B/1774